Be

Laura

D0422958

vsxx

Mcoo

On the Birth of Your Child

Also by Sherry Conway Appel

Wisdom from the Kitchen

From Mother to Daughter:
Advice and Lessons for a Good Life

Thanks, Mom

On the Birth of Your Child

Words of Wisdom from Mother to Daughter

Sherry Conway Appel

ST. MARTIN'S PRESS ❧ NEW YORK

ON THE BIRTH OF YOUR CHILD: WORDS OF WISDOM FROM
MOTHER TO DAUGHTER. Copyright © 1999 by Allen Appel
and Sherry Conway Appel. All rights reserved. Printed in the
United States of America. No part of this book may be used
or reproduced in any manner whatsoever without written
permission except in the case of brief quotations embodied
in critical articles or reviews. For information, address
St. Martin's Press, 175 Fifth Avenue, New York, N.Y. 10010

Library of Congress Cataloging-in-Publication Data

Appel, Sherry Conway.
    On the birth of your child: words of wisdom from
mother to daughter / Sherry Conway Appel.
        p.   cm.
    ISBN 0-312-20690-9
    1. Childbirth Miscellanea.   2. Interpersonal relations
Miscellanea.   3. Mothers and daughters.   I. Title.
RG652.A66   1999
649'.122—dc21
                                        99–36065
                                          CIP

First Edition: November 1999

10   9   8   7   6   5   4   3   2   1

For Allen Reuben Appel,
and in memory of Leo John Conway,
two wonderful fathers

On the Birth of
Your Child

A Mother's Love

Holding your baby in your arms for the very first time is an experience you will never forget. The feelings rush over you—amazement, wonder, love, satisfaction, fear, and the enormity of your new responsibility for this young creature.

Caring for this child, coaxing it, teaching it, loving it, has now become the principal force in your life. And since babies don't come with instructions, guidance must come from those around you. Most probably your first teacher will be your mother.

I always knew I wanted children because I could see the joy that my mother gained from the task of raising us. There were five in our family, and I thought the experience of being around them and my many nieces and nephews as they were born would provide me with the "natural" ability to mother I saw in my own mom.

I was wrong, of course. I quickly learned that taking care of others' children is vastly different from minding your own. No longer can you turn the baby over to Mom when you want to go swimming or read a book. You and the baby's father are the ones who are responsible now, and there's usually no one else willing to feed the baby in the wee hours or provide you with an answer to your most immediate questions. No one, that is, except for your own mother or mother-in-law, new grandmas usually more than ready and eager to lend a hand or two and offer advice.

In my own house, things didn't quite work out the way I planned. My mother died before I conceived my first child, so I didn't have the benefit of her guiding words. There were many desperate hours when I longed to turn to her for help. Instead, I managed by remembering how she handled things, what she said to me when we were cooing over her latest grandchild, what my many sisters passed along.

We never had a chance to have that all-important conversation about child rearing. But if we had, I think I know at least a few of the things she would have told me:

Love your children with all your might.

Honor each of your children as individuals.

Allow them to make mistakes, but always be there for comfort and to help pick up the pieces.

Recognize all of their traits, good and bad, but focus on the good; nurturing, coaxing, and praising.

Always give them a chance—they will probably surprise you.

Hug them often.

Tell them you love them.

This is how she and my father raised me, my little brother John, and my three sisters, Barbara, Susan, and Judy. This is what I have done with my own two children, Leah and Charlie, at night when I tuck them into bed with plenty of kisses and a whispered "I love you. Good night."

—*Sherry Conway Appel*

Getting Started: Pregnancy

$\mathcal{T}$o my dear daughter,

Your father and I tried to have children for several years but were unsuccessful. Two weeks after the doctors told us we would never have a child, we discovered I was already pregnant with your brother. What a shock!

In April of 1998 we had defied the odds by becoming pregnant again. While the doctors scratched their heads in disbelief, your father and I sent up silent thanks to God. I have chosen the name Faith because I once read, "Faith is the substance of things hoped for."

As I write this letter you are still growing inside my womb. When you push one of your tiny limbs against my belly, I am reminded what a miracle you are.

Here are some promises I am making to you, my dear daughter.

I promise to listen to your heart song. To me, this means knowing the essence of you.

I will take the time to really know you and encourage all that is good in you.

I will see you for the unique, special person that you are.

I will hold dear to me all that you hold dear to you.

I will try never to embarrass you.

I will not ridicule you.

I will try not to compare you to others.

I will always love you.

—*Leah Marie Brown*

Pregnancy, childbirth, and parenting are three of life's great adventures. Try and remember to enjoy the ride as you go up and down the mountains.

As soon as you think you are pregnant, go to your obstetrician. If you don't know a good one, ask your family or friends. If you're new in town, go to the playground and talk to the new moms; they'll have plenty to say. Go to a doctor who has a lot of experience; when you are in the delivery room and a problem arises, you want someone who's been there before.

Buy a couple of basic baby books—ones by Dr. Benjamin Spock and Penelope Leach are good. You'll use them all the time.

Every pregnancy is different, just as every child is different.

"If a chimpanze can do it without reading a book, so can you."
—*Teresa Chin Jones*

"They didn't have birth classes when my mom was pregnant with me, but I recommend them. When it comes down to your time, however, everything can be totally different from the way you learned it in class. The perfect 'No Drugs, Natural Labor' is not always, or even often, possible. Don't feel guilty if your delivery doesn't go as perfectly as it does in class. Believe me, it won't."
—*Sally Brickman*

Practice your breathing exercises. What seems silly at home and in class can be extremely useful when you really need it.

"Every mother likes to tell you the story of their baby's birth. It's a bonding experience and no one can resist. Just don't pay too much attention to the awful ones. Instead, smile and nod your head. Pretty soon you'll have your own stories to frighten expectant mothers with."
—*Ingrid Barth*

Listen to everyone's advice. You can reject what you don't like, but your thinking about things will change after the baby is born. You never know what will be useful then.

Get all the sleep you need now—and read all the novels and go to all the current movies—because once the baby comes, you'll be lucky if you have enough time to watch the dryer turn.

If you didn't start taking folic acid supplements before you became pregnant, start immediately. Take 0.4 mg a day. Even though many foods contain folic acid, you can't be sure you're getting enough without the supplement.

If you have trouble taking the pre-natal vitamins your doctor prescribes, ask for another brand. They aren't all the same and some are easier to tolerate than others. Remember, it's taking them that counts.

*Eat lots of fiber—oatmeal, bran flakes, legumes; it
makes the iron in the baby vitamins easier to
tolerate, and you'll feel better, too.*

"My husband and I were both working when we decided it was time to have kids. When I told my mom, she asked which one of us was going to quit and stay home with the baby. At first it made me mad, but I told myself it was just because she was from a different generation. But after a year of trying to juggle two careers and a baby we decided that she was right. Now my husband stays home with our little girl and it is better for all of us, even though we have a lot less money.

"It's not always possible, I know, but try it. All other arrangements are substitutes for parental care. You can try to fool yourself, you can rationalize all you want, you can read the studies, you can tap dance on your head, but it won't change anything. A two-parent home is the best family. A nonworking parent, mother or father, is still the best person to raise your child. You have to give up a lot, but you gain much more in return."

—*Shelly Heller*

*Buy one great pregnancy outfit and borrow the rest
from friends.*

*Keep your options open about child care. Many a
career woman has changed her mind once her baby
is in her arms. Consider all the options now, and
then use your family leave to make your decision.
Your feelings may change and part-time work may
look more attractive.*

*Don't be ashamed to ask other parents for hand-
me-downs when you're getting ready for the baby.
They're usually glad to pass things along. Babies
grow out of clothing before they wear out their
clothing.*

"My husband and I had decided against following the family custom of naming our first-born boy William, the same name as my father and his father and his father before him. My husband was out of town when I went into labor so my mom drove me to the hospital. In between labor pains she started the conversation with the words, 'It would make your father happy if you would . . .' and I knew I was doomed. William it was. But many years in the future, when son William's wife is going to have a baby, I'll probably do the same thing to him."

—*Beth Bester*

"In the last two months of my pregnancy, I could hardly sleep. I guess it was good training for the months to come. One thing that made it easier, however, was the small baby-sized pillow I bought. I used it to prop and support my belly at night when I slept on my side, and it worked like a charm."

—*Sherry Conway Appel*

During pregnancy, sleep on your left side. It's easier on the heart. During the last few months, try not to sleep on your back, since the baby will be pressing down on the main veins into your legs.

Find a pediatrician with whom you are comfortable—do they have a morning calling period where you can ask questions and express concerns before having to bring the baby in? Do they have a separate place in the waiting room for well baby visits and sick babies? Do they mind questions— and do they respond adequately to them or do they shrug them off? Try and visit one or two before the baby is born—ask other parents. Everyone will tell you if they like or hate their pediatrician.

Schedule your prenatal doctor visits so you and your husband can go together.

Buy a video camera if you don't have one. You and your child will watch the tapes your entire life. Learn to use it before the baby comes; that way you won't miss those milestones while trying to figure out how to operate the camera.

Expect to change your mind about the kind of diaper you're going to use. Many people start out with cloth because of worries about the environment, but disposables are a lot easier. Don't feel guilty if you change your mind. You'll feel guilty enough about a thousand other things, so don't let this issue get to you.

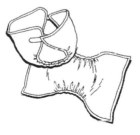

"Be careful being around puppies when you're pregnant. Your maternal instincts are in high gear then and you'll be tempted to take home a cute little puppy. You'll be sorry if you do."

—*Eileen Toumonoff*

Don't be the family member who changes the cat litter. It can release toxins that are harmful to the baby. Assign that job to someone else.

Try to figure out all the cruel nicknames that can be made out of a name before you choose it.

Decide whether or not your baby is going to be circumcised before you go to the hospital. You won't be thinking clearly once you're in labor and this is an important decision. Recent studies show that there are no health benefits to either the child or future partners to being circumcised.

"From the first day of pregnancy, I saved every lucky penny I found and put it in the baby's bank."

—*Kirsten Burton*

"At the time of my thirty-seventh week I went for a doctor's visit. The doctor said I was three centimeters dilated and I could have my baby at any time now, but it could be weeks before anything happened. She told me to go home and have sex, and that would trigger regular contractions. She said that having sex and having orgasms would trigger a faster labor. So I did. I went home and had sex. I had orgasms. And that night I went into labor."

—*Catie Babb*

Unless told differently by your doctor, you don't have to restrict your salt intake when pregnant.

Having a few drinks before you knew you were pregnant isn't going to put your baby at risk. But after you know, don't drink at all.

"Morning sickness quite frequently occurs more than just in the morning, and on average does not go away by the third month. One type, hyperemesis gravidarum, can be quite serious and debilitating—I know, I had it for both of my pregnancies, as did my mother and my grandmother. Some doctors will make light of this problem or even make your morning sickness almost seem like it's your own fault. It's not. There are things that can be done."

—*Juanita Patterson*

Keep crackers by your bedside. If you wake up feeling a little nauseous, munch on a few and rest a minute while your stomach settles. It makes getting up easier.

If you smoke, quit. If anyone in your household smokes, make them quit or don't allow them to smoke in the house. Secondhand smoke has now been linked to low birthweight and numerous health problems in babies. Even using a nicotine patch is preferable to exposing your baby to the thousands of other toxins in the cigarette smoke.

"When I was pregnant with my first child and taking a walk with my wonderful Scotch-Irish Appalachian grandmother, she said, 'Don't step over the pennyroyal plant, it's bad luck for a pregnant woman.' Many years later as an herbalist, I found that pennyroyal can cause abortions. I don't think my grandmother ever knew that fact. She just had that piece of oral lore from her foremothers."

—*Linda Ours Rago*

The Hospital and Birth

From the moment you arrive in labor, make friends with the nurses. It can make a big difference.

"Even with all the things that you read and all the advice that someone can give you, you can't really appreciate giving birth until you go through it yourself. It kind of gives new meaning to the word *hindsight*."

—Leanne Whiteman

"Here's one thing I'm going to tell my daughter for sure when she gets pregnant. Never eat a huge meal of Mexican food several hours before going into labor. That's what I did, and I can assure you that it was a mistake."

—*Victoria Harper*

Epidural pumps are the latest in self-medicating during childbirth. Ask your doctor before you get to the hospital to prescribe one for you so it will be available should you need it.

"I decided I wasn't going to be one of those women who yelled in childbirth. So when the time came, I sang—'The Ohio State Fight Song'—loud and clear. My husband told me I was off-key. I have shared this with my daughters and they have done the same."

—*Sally Games*

"After you have the baby, you forget about the pain."

—*Beverly Warfield*

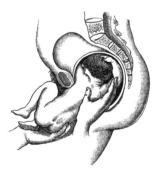

"Once you've had the baby, don't take time to count the toes and fingers. As soon as you get the baby in your arms, let it latch on to your breast and nurse right away in the delivery room. There's not any milk yet, but a baby learns more quickly to suck that way and it makes breast feeding easier later."

—*Tracy Weins*

*Breast-feeding is best, but it may not come
naturally. Ask your doctor or hospital for the name
of a lactation expert and call them before the baby
is born. The first forty-eight hours after birth are
often critical to the success of breastfeeding—for
both mom and child—and it's often the time when
you are most stressed. So try and work out the
assistance before you have the baby!
La Leche League moms provide great support and
guidance. Remember, each baby is different; some
seem to catch on immediately, others have to be
taught. Don't give up!*

*Your breasts will be rock hard when your milk
comes in, usually twelve to twenty hours or so after
birth. Put hot washcloths on them about ten
minutes before the baby nurses so they will soften
and the baby can latch on easier.*

"I was told walking while having contractions would ease the pain. It didn't help."

—*Stacy Jordan*

"When I was in the hospital having my second child, the woman in the bed next to me was celebrating the birth of her first. And I mean celebrating! She had family and friends there almost constantly, never really got to spend time alone with the baby, and went home exhausted. Although it is natural to want to show off the baby to all, try to limit your visitors or at least the visiting hours. Use that quiet time to watch and hold your baby. With such short hospital stays now, this should be cherished time. Use it wisely."

—*Sherry Conway Appel*

"My mom told me that when I was born I started coming before the doctor had got to the hospital so the nurses tied her legs together with a bedsheet to make sure I didn't arrive before he did. Can you imagine the lawsuits today? Mom stayed in the hospital a full five days and was returned home in an ambulance. All this was common procedure in those days. Only hospital workers were allowed in the delivery room. When my granddaughter was born recently, everyone and his brother was invited in to watch and videotape."

—*Sunday Wynkoop*

Use the experience of the nurses. They know all the tricks on how to diaper, dress, and feed the baby.

Prepare for some bleeding for about seven to ten days after the birth. If you need more than an average number of pads, however, call the doctor.

Tearing and stitches do hurt. Be sure and take two or three sitz baths every day after birth and not only will you feel better, you will mend faster. There are gadgets you can place in the toilet bowl that make it easier and quicker to prepare, so you can take one every time the baby sleeps. You might be so caught up in the baby that you forget. But this is for you. It may seem like a chore, but it will make sitting down much more comfortable.

Get out of bed and walk around as soon as you can (and the doctor says it's okay). Even though it will hurt and you'll be sore, you'll heal faster and feel better sooner.

Take a roll of soft toilet paper to the hospital. It's much more comfortable than the institutional stuff.

"When I was having labor pains, two things helped me feel a little better: putting a warm towel on my stomach and taking a hot shower."
—*Tonya Stewart*

"My husband got so excited when the baby finally came out that he jumped up into the air and cut his finger on the overhead light. There was a lot of bleeding and for a few minutes everyone pretty much forgot about me and the baby."
—*Cina Radler*

*If you're going to have your baby circumcised,
request analgesia for the procedure. One simple but
effective method is to give the baby a sugar-soaked
pacifier. Doctors don't know why it works,
but it does.*

"On my fiftieth birthday my mother sent me the
receipt for my birth at Dr. Moore's Hospital. It
really meant a lot to me. Two hundred dollars for
two weeks!"
—*Mary Jane Kolar*

*Save the newspaper from the day of the baby's birth
to show the child years later what life was like the
day she was born.*

"I was the number-two child. When my mother was in labor with me, the doctor came into check her and decided I would not be born for several more hours. He went home and his nurse went to the movies. I decided to come and was delivered by the intern.

"When my second child was ready to be born, I decided I was in labor so went to the hospital. The resident checked me and said he would keep me but I was not in labor. One hour later our son was born. Instead of the resident delivering our son, I panted with each contraction until the doctor could get there. He told me he got lost on the way to the hospital."

—*Susan Conway Himes*

Don't be afraid to ask questions of the nurses.
When you're learning about caring for your baby,
no question's too simple or stupid to ask.

"I have told my daughter what *not* to do when you're pregnant. I was a classic type A. During the summer of 1973, I was studying for my doctoral orals, working full time, caring for my three-year-old son, and was pregnant with my second child. I was so task-oriented that when I began leaking fluid at the beginning of my seventh month, I just stuck Turkish towels between my legs and continued to study. After all, the baby wasn't due for two months, but my doctoral orals were scheduled. I actually went through the orals with the towels between my legs! Once told I had passed, I announced that I was in labor and was taken to the hospital. My daughter Samantha was born seven and a half weeks early. Luckily there was no harm done, but it was definitely *not* the right thing to do!"

—*Lynne Glassman*

Watch the nurses carefully when they give your new baby a bath at the hospital. This is something you'll want to remember the first time you try it at home!

Just because your first-born was by Caesarian section, it doesn't mean your second must be as well. Depending on circumstances, you can have a "natural" delivery if you and your doctor agree it's safe.

"After delivery, you will be handed your baby. This is the most precious moment you will ever spend with your newborn. After nine months of wondering what she looked like, sounded like, and even smelled like, now is your chance to look into those sweet little eyes.

"Today delivery rooms are not limited to just the parents, and I could have had my whole extended family (and a few strangers) in the room if I wanted. Thankfully, I chose only to have my husband with me. I say thankfully because I would not have wanted to share those first few precious moments with anyone else."

—*Christine Middleton*

First Weeks

My mom came to help out after our first daughter, Tracey, was born. The first night we were home from the hospital Mom told me to sleep through the night and she would get up and feed Tracey. So off to bed I went. About two A.M. Tracey began to cry. I woke up and waited for Mom to get her. After about seven minutes I decided I'd better get up and take care of the baby. I went in the kitchen and fixed the bottle and sat down in the chair next to Mom who was sleeping on the couch in the living room. After

Tracey finished her bottle, I put her back to bed and went back to sleep. About seven A.M. Tracey and I both woke up and went to see Mom in the living room. Mom was just waking up. When she saw us she said, 'What a good baby. She slept through the night!' I just laughed and said, 'She didn't, Mom—you did!' "

—*Deborah Herr*

Always put the baby to sleep on its back. Never put it on its stomach. *Make sure everyone in the family knows this and any babysitters know it as well.*

Babies aren't as fragile as you think. Be careful, but don't be afraid.

Hold your baby as much as possible and as much as you want. You can't spoil her. Holding and comforting your baby makes for secure children and confident, independent adults.

"When our daughter Mikell was born we scrawled the following message on the blackboard in the kitchen:

'When the baby cries, check:
- Is she hungry?
- Does she need to be changed?
- Does she need to be burped?
- Hold her!' "

—*Donna Belser*

The best way to burp a baby: Position the baby either at your shoulder or sit it up on your lap. Don't pat its back. Instead, gently rub its back from the bottom up. And be sure to throw a cloth over you!

Postpartum blues are very real. Expect to feel sad a couple of days after the birth as your hormones sweep through your body. It passes. If you can't shake them, talk to your doctor. Don't be ashamed to get help.

Never shake your baby. No matter how tired you are; no matter how angry you are. Your baby's life is in your hands.

Don't ever heat baby bottles in the microwave. The liquid can heat unevenly and burn the baby.

Lack of sleep makes you irritable—remember that when your baby starts crying. Try taking three deep breaths and counting to ten.

Don't expect your husband to be a klutz when it comes to dealing with the baby. He may surprise you and be just as good at it as you are.

New babies can see, hear, and smell very well. They focus most clearly on objects eight to ten inches from them, so that's where you should position yourself when interacting with them.

"When my first boy was born, my mother was far away in Ireland. But my landlady was very helpful to me. When visitors came to see the baby she'd tell them I was resting. In those days people liked to take a baby by the hands and lift him up. You can hurt a baby that way, so she'd stand by the bassinet and tell every visitor, 'Look, but don't touch!'"

—*Jean Kelly McCall*

Before you or anyone else picks up the new baby, wash your hands!

There are many monitoring gadgets on the market today. Probably the simplest and most inexpensive is a baby minder. You put the monitor in the baby's room and take the receiver with you when you travel through the house. It really helps your peace of mind when you've got work to do elsewhere.

"Rather than more gifts for the baby, tell your friends you need a 'pamper package'—bath, lotion, loofa—anything to help you relax once you come home. It's a great gift to the new mother, especially from your business colleagues."
—*Mary Jane Kolar*

Buy several pairs of disposable underwear for the first few weeks when you're home from the hospital. Yours won't be ruined that way.

*you and your husband are both totally
...capacitated, resist offers of live-in help from either
your mom or your husband's mom the first week.
It's a tough but wonderful week, and you both need
that time to bond with your baby.*

*Despite the obvious, cloth diapers have many uses.
They make excellent burp cloths for your shoulders.
Also, cut them up and use them as nursing bra pads;
they're cheaper, washable, and reusable.*

*Jot down any questions you have as you think of
them (otherwise you won't remember). Take the
list to your first week's well-baby visit with the
pediatrician. Have your hubby or mom write down
the answers as you hear them, so you'll both
remember.*

"My mother came to visit and was diapering the baby with Pampers, which had just come on the market. When she was finished, she flushed the diaper down the toilet. Of course, it immediately stopped up the toilet and there was water everywhere. My husband was so mad!"

—*Sandy Fisher*

A baby's stomach is about the size of a golf ball. Expect frequent feedings that do not necessarily occur on a schedule.

"When my first was born, I said to my mother, 'I can handle it, you don't have to stay over the first night home from the hospital.' After the first sleepless night I called her at eight A.M. 'Help! Come over!' Of course she did immediately and stayed as long as I needed her. Mothers are great because they care and can help with your more personal concerns like stitches, soreness, and constipation. Just hearing, 'Oh I remember . . . ' is comforting and reassuring."

—*Linda Ours Rago*

"My mother told me that the directions for caring for a baby were the same ones found on the top of a mayonnaise jar: Keep Cool!"

—*Mary Jane Kolar*

Before the umbilical cord falls off, use a side-snap shirt instead of a onesie. This will help the cord dry and fall off sooner.

Don't make your house "too quiet" when the baby sleeps during the day. This way they won't become light sleepers and will be able to sleep better in various situations.

"We had gotten up at 3 A.M. We left the Children's Home and after a four-hour flight arrived in Moscow where we were staying. Sonya and Matthew, our new children, quickly realized that a kitchen in a home is quite different from an orphanage; one could get food just by asking for it! They tried on every piece of clothing we had with us, broke a lamp and a large vase, and pulled the toilet string from the ceiling. We walked to the park and had a hard time convincing them they must hold our hands when walking along or crossing busy streets.

"By nine o'clock that evening, I sat down in our little cramped room and cried. I was exhausted, I felt how much responsibility lay ahead of us, but most of all I was happy. After nine years of marriage we finally had two beautiful children. Then I felt two little bodies climbing onto my lap to console me. My husband rubbed my shoulders. That feeling of a family and of caring and love just added to my emotional overload and I cried harder—out of happiness!"

—*Paivi Spoon*

"I have always told my grown daughters that a daddy needs to bond early as it pays off later on in life. In my own home, as I cooked dinner, my husband's evening pleasure was to walk around the block where he visited with all the other mothers. They would exchange news such as: teeth (how many), fevers (how high), favorite foods, weights, etc. When he came home, he shared news about other children and the neighborhood gossip. From the beginning of their lives he was a good listener, and his role never changed for my daughters."

—*Mary Catherine Walker*

A good mother knows that the father should be involved in all aspects of a child's life. Don't shut him out because it's "women's work." It's parents' work.

"Disposable bottles. There's no other way to go if you're not breast-feeding. Breast may be best, but not everyone can do it."
—*Linda Wilson*

Breast-feeding does not make you retain or gain weight. In fact, it helps burn calories.

If you're breast-feeding, drink plenty of water.

You save around five hundred dollars per year by breast-feeding.

"Pay the extra and buy a *double* breast pump—it'll save you a lot of time."

—*Kirsten Burton*

Put a baby safety pin on your bra strap so you'll know which breast the baby last nursed. Always start the next feeding with that breast since it will probably have more milk.

Keep your fingernails short and wash your hands often to keep germs at a minimum.

"When my first child was born, I was completely overwhelmed. What was I supposed to do with this baby? I called my mother and started crying. 'I'm incompetent,' I wailed.

"She told me to pack up the baby's things and come to her house. 'You need time so you can understand that you already know everything you need to know,' she told me.

"The first night I was with my parents I nursed Nick, and put him in his little travel crib. He wailed.

"My parents sat down to dinner as if nothing special was happening. 'How can you eat while this is going on?' I pleaded.

"My mother looked at me, calmly swallowed her food, and said, 'Believe me, we've heard worse.'

"That night was a turning point for me. With her simple statement, my mother gave me the most precious of gifts—perspective. Babies cried. They just did. You did what you could, and then you let *them* work it out. The only thing I absolutely had

to do was love my baby. And that was easy."
—*Robin Latham*

Buy a calendar and keep it near where you feed the baby. That way you can jot down observations, or any other little thing as it happens. This can be useful when asking the doctor questions. And it's great fun to look at in later years.

"Before making the decision to go back to work, it helps to recognize that even if you choose to stay home, it's not forever. Usually five to ten years will take care of two or three kids in their most critical years. During that time, it's still possible to get more education or do some part-time work."
—*Teresa Chin Jones*

You can't spoil a baby. If they cry, pick them up.

All babies want to be held and be close to you. If you want your hands free, get a Snugli and wear it while you do your housework or your job work.

"My daughter was five weeks premature but at five pounds, she was able to come home from the hospital with me right away. She was so tiny, her arms would only come halfway down her sleeves! She spent the next two months being held and cuddled, either on my chest or on her dad's. We've since learned that this closeness and involvement are the best stimulation you can provide for a premie."

—*Sherry Conway Appel*

Yard sales are great for bargain-priced and mostly-new baby clothes.

Always wash all clothes—both new and used—in a mild detergent like Dreft before you use them. It takes out the sizing and ensures there are no allergic reactions.

Remember when buying a diaper bag that your husband will be carrying it, too. Unisex is better.

Diaper bags can now be disguised as backpacks. Make sure to find one with a good diaper changing pad included.

"The best gadget you can buy (or receive) is a baby swing. It really saves you when you need to cook, clean, or otherwise need two hands. Just don't be tempted to use it too often."
—Susan DeWit

Don't bathe your baby by immersing her until the umbilical cord dries up and falls off, usually between five days and three weeks. Give her a sponge bath instead.

There's nothing like the smell and the feel of a little baby fresh from his bath. Buy one of those hooded towels to keep him warm while you're drying him.

Newborns are extremely portable and they sleep a lot. Go out to dinner or even take a trip if you feel like it. But movies may be pushing it.

"Don't spend the big bucks on a fancy stroller. I found myself using the inexpensive umbrella stroller 90 percent of the time. And get a baby backpack. I cooked, vacuumed, and did almost everything with the baby on my back."

—*Regina M. Smith*

Take naps whenever you can.

The baby doesn't see that the house isn't perfectly clean. The baby sees the mother.

Trust your intuition. If you feel your baby should be seen by the doctor for a problem, take her to the doctor.

A great toy for a newborn is something called Double Feature. It has a baby-safe mirror on one side and black and white pictures on the other. Put it on the changing table or side of the crib and watch the baby laugh.

"I can't say I was very close to my mum, but when I got pregnant during the first year of my marriage it got me and my mum talking about things we never had talked about before. After I had the baby I went to her house for three weeks and I'd tell everyone I know to do the same. First of all, it is a big help: You don't have to worry about dinner, or sitting for ages with people who come to visit. I used to excuse myself and Mum would sit with them. She taught me everything, from bathing to feeding. One reason I'm really glad I had my baby is that it made my mum my friend."

—*Dina Tabbah*

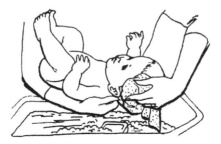

"My first baby was off the colic scale. He cried nonstop, did not want to be held, did not want to be put down either. He rolled over as a newborn not because he wanted to but because he thrashed so much. When my second was born, I became very upset about my new baby's behavior. I called my mom and told her that I thought Mathew had brain damage. I explained that the baby cried very little, slept a lot, and was not too terribly active. My mom said, 'That's not mental retardation, that's normal!' I have since had three more children. Each of the five has his or her own distinct and separate personality."

—*Susan Cross*

You can't do much to stop colic—just hug them and hold them close and try to block out their crying. Eventually it will go away on its own. Try to remember—it's not the baby's fault, and it's not yours. Here are some tricks that may or may not work: Lay the baby on a blanket on the top of a running clothes dryer and cuddle him there (never take your hands off him). Run the vacuum cleaner near his crib. Tune a nearby radio to white static and leave it on. Sometimes an unusual sound soothes them. If all else fails, put them in the car and start driving.

"My mom told me to try to keep my sense of humor after the baby was born. My husband and I were on our first trip with the baby and she had been crying for an hour. We'd tried everything with no luck. The crying was driving us insane. After crying at what we thought was peak volume, Emma doubled her efforts to new heights. My husband began to laugh in amazement at our tiny daughter. I found myself joining in. We laughed so hard we had to pull off the road. I'm sure it was hysteria on our part, but we laughed until we cried.

"And of course the baby, for whatever reason, stopped crying.

"Mom was right. Try to find your sense of humor again. It's still there—you just have to work a little to rekindle it."

—*Sandy Fisher*

"Right after each of my girls was born, I made up a song that included her own name. I would sing her song to her often and she would begin to recognize that this was her mommy's very special gift to her. I would get the greatest joy when I would come home from work or shopping, sneak up on one of them, and surprise her by singing her song. To see their faces light up was awesome."

—*Shirley Posten*

First Year

$\mathcal{T}$he one thing my children have taught me is patience!"

—*Cina Radler*

Read to your baby, sing to your baby, dance with your baby.

Just because a baby doesn't know what you're saying doesn't mean she doesn't enjoy the sound of your voice. Talk to them throughout the day; it's good company for both of you.

You may have good friends who have teenage children. That doesn't mean that those children are going to make good babysitters.

Always ask about any medicine your doctor prescribes.

Even if your baby seems hungry, don't feed him solids (no cereal, fruit, etc.) until at least six months. You will be tempted after three months and other mothers will tell you it's okay. This is when food allergies can first arise, however, so it is better to wait.

Good baby food is just good regular food mashed up. You can do it yourself. The regular stuff in the little jars is convenient, but expensive.

Babies need fat in their diets. Don't feed your baby low-fat or nonfat foods just because you think she's too chubby.

"For every grandchild, I've made a baby quilt, usually out of some fabric I used to make clothes for their mother when she was young. I put their name and mine linked together in a heart, so as they grow, they'll always know I love them."

—*Irene Appel*

Colorful plastic chain links are ideal for attaching to the crib, stroller, or high chair. They'll help keep the baby occupied and, as they grow, will help develop finger dexterity.

When your child starts sitting in the high chair and begins to eat real food, give her some Cheerios or other soft food she can feed herself with her hands while you feed her the real thing by spoon. She can satisfy her curiosity with the food and you can feel comfortable that she is getting some nourishment.

One-piece blanket sleepers are perfect for cool bedrooms. They're a little heavier than regular sleepers and zip up the front. You don't have to worry about the baby moving out from under the blankets. They all have non-skid feet in them for when the baby starts to pull himself up and cruise around.

"When our son Jesse was born, my husband and I determined not to become 'parent-geeks.' These are people who buy every baby accessory they can get their hands on in the hopes it will help them raise their child without effort and without making any stupid mistakes, while sending the baby's I.Q. into the low 200s. So when a friend gave us a gadget that held two small bottles on a cold side and had a side that you plugged to heat the bottles, I was against it. A Yuppie contraption, I thought. This was before I learned what it was like to be awakened at one A.M., then again at three, then again at five, in order to hike from our bedroom on the third floor to the kitchen on the first floor, heat the water in a pan, then climb back up to the bedroom. This hot/cold gadget became more than an indulgence; it was a necessity."

—*Lorrie Kahaner*

Ninety percent of a baby's brain development occurs during the first three years. It's your job to keep the baby stimulated.

All babies develop physically and emotionally at their own pace. Don't worry if yours doesn't adhere to the schedules and charts in baby books or to the proud claims of other mothers. If your doctor says the baby is fine, then the baby is fine.

Don't sit little babies in front of the TV set, even for those shows that are made for infants. Do something with them. Read, sing, play, dance. It may seem like too much for a busy mother, but remember they will only be this small once.

"My friend Donna's baby was born six weeks before mine. She started walking at nine months. When my daughter was still creeping like a monkey at fourteen months, my mother-in-law told me not to worry. 'How many children have you seen going to school on their hands and knees? She'll catch up.' Of course she did and I learned a good lesson. Never compare your child to anyone else's or to another of your own. If you're worried about their development, ask your pediatrician."

—*Sherry Conway Appel*

Fresh air is one of the best ways to cure diaper rash.
But keep a diaper handy, just in case!

Yes, there is a difference between boy and girl babies—get the right diaper for their needs and you'll have fewer messes. Also, keep a diaper or cloth handy when you are changing your little boy. Otherwise, you'll be cleaning off the wall and yourself too!

"At some point you expect them to start sleeping through the night. I don't think mine ever did. Maybe they did when they went to college, but I don't know."

—*Edmina Janus*

Make sure you visit all family child care homes several times. Most you'll reject after one visit, but if you like a place, ask if you can drop in unannounced and then do it. This sounds obvious and simple but you'll be surprised at how long finding child care takes. Don't rush into anything.

If you're looking at family child-care homes and all the kids are sitting around watching TV, forget that one. Special videos can be fine, Sesame Street is a godsend, but too much of any of it is not good for your child.

"I realized after I became a mother that I was now willing to pick up *anything* with my bare hand."
—*Regina M. Smith*

Get yourself a cordless phone. You can talk and keep tabs on a crawling child at the same time, do chores, and move around in general.

"Read, read, read to your baby. Start when she's a newborn and continue until they're old enough to read to themselves, and then both of you read to each other. We never put our kids to bed without reading or telling a story. My mother read to me when I was little and some of my fondest memories are laughing and whacking my dad to wake him up when he fell asleep while he was reading to us. Which he always did."

—*Sandy Fisher*

Buy some sturdy little cardboard books—the simpler the better—that they can hold onto. Make a game out of finding the animals in the pictures and using words. It's much too early to expect them to learn to read the words: Instead, they are learning valuable vocabulary. The joy of closeness and having them on your laps are nice benefits, too. But don't be surprised or alarmed if they chew on the edges!

"When my daughter was about two to three months old, I'd sit her in her car seat or other baby seat so she could see out a window. She loved to look at the trees, the occasional bird, the sunshine. It often gave me time to get little chores done and kept her quietly stimulated. She's still incredibly observant. I like to think it started here."

—*Susan Kleimann*

"Play and sing lots of music—in our case soft rock and classical. I believe this led to my son's future interest in music."

—*Ann Pellerin*

Keep two diaper bags packed; one for quicker trips, another for the day care or sitter.

"Buy a small suitcase and keep it in the car for emergencies—fill it with extra baby clothes, diapers, lotions, powder, washcloth, baby wipes, blanket, sweater. You will be surprised how often you use it. Just remember to replenish it and update it with the change of seasons and the growth of the child."

—*Lavonne Proctor*

Babies don't need shoes until they start walking—between twelve and eighteen months.

Here's the story on toys: Girls usually prefer dolls, boys like trucks. It doesn't work to try and force a child of any age to take up a toy he or she is not interested in, no matter how firm your unisex convictions are.

Get down on their level. If you put the baby on the floor, get on the floor to play with her.

Keep index cards handy to write down things your kids say or do. You may think you won't forget, but you do. The cards are fun to go back and read later. They can be added to baby books, as well.

A cool mist humidifier cuts down on colds or can help clear them up quickly.

"When I was small, I desperately wanted a baby sister. My mother often reminds me of the time I informed her that my baby brother might not really be a boy. We might have made a mistake."
—Anne Ridgely

You may not love what they do, but always love them!

Break the habit, not the child.

Let your kids know their grandparents.

Being a mom is a special privilege—enjoy it!

Second Year

$\mathcal{F}$or the first three years of our daughter's life, I was a stay-at-home mom. My daughter Nina and I would play together at a table in her room and if the phone would ring or there was another interruption, I would excuse myself to go and take care of it. A friend remarked on my saying 'Please excuse me' to my toddler. I told my friend that I thought if you expected children to have good manners, you had to model good manners. I believe I was right. My thirty-year-old daughter has beautiful manners!"

—*Beverly Silverberg*

"Please" and "thank you" start now. If you say it to them, they'll say it back to you.

Try not to say "no" too quickly.

As children get more independent, they want to make more decisions. What to wear for the day— even what pair of socks to wear—can be a real struggle of wills, particularly when you're in a hurry or have an appointment. The trick is to provide your child with a choice. The night before, you pick out two outfits. Then offer your child the choice of either one. She feels in control and you don't have the power struggle.

"Our daughter was one of those kids who was slow to develop motor skills. When other kids were up and walking she was scooting along in a weird crawl. I took her to Gymboree. She crawled around through all sorts of great equipment and had fun. I believe it helped her tremendously. Gymboree had just started back then, but now they're everywhere. Just look in the phone book."
—*Alison Frank*

Must haves at all times (keep some in the diaper bag, too): raisins, Cheerios, small packages of apple juice, pretzels, Goldfish crackers.

Start a habit of eating dinner together as a family as soon as possible.

"My daughter was a fussy eater and I was always worried she wasn't getting enough to eat. So I began cooking with her. I'd give her an apron to wear and she would pour and stir for me. We'd make banana bread and she would eat the bananas. I'd make an apple pie and she would help roll out the extra pie dough and make 'special' cookies with sugar and cinnamon. She always ate the final product, as well, proud that she helped."

—*Sherry Conway Appel*

"Eating in a restaurant with my one-year-old daughter can sometimes be a serious problem. By the time we've ordered, she usually gets bored and starts making noise and fussing. My husband's family saved us by making my daughter her own 'Going Out to Dinner Purse.' It contains four little books, small Playskool people, and crayons. She loves carrying her special purse since it makes her feel like 'Big People.' "

—*Tracy Weins*

The simpler the toy, the better. Little children neither want nor respond to complexity.

Get down on your hands and knees and crawl around the house. You'll be amazed at what you'll see a toddler can get into.

Once your baby starts crawling, insert baby-proof plugs in all your unused outlets and child proof all your cabinets with baby-proof hinges. It takes a bit of time, but it will pay off in safety. Hinges and plugs are available at most grocery stores and pharmacies.

"When my sister was three, my grandmother took her to the beauty parlor. Debbie had naturally bright red, long straight hair, but when she came home, it was very short and *very* curly. She looked just like Bozo the Clown. My mother was horrified. She always told my sister and I when our babies were born, 'Don't let your grandmother take the baby to get its hair cut!' "

—*Marilyn Rybak*

A baby can get bored pretty quickly in a playpen. Set up one room of the house that she can't get out of and rigorously screen it for anything that can hurt her. Then let her maneuver around and explore on her own.

"Things I wish I had when my children were young that I now use for my grandchild: slip-proof plastic bath tub; Bouncee jumping chair that hangs in the doorway; winter clothing and blankets made out of polar fleece—warm, cozy, lightweight, and washable; and a camcorder."
                                      —*Marita Jane Brown*

Always put a baby gate up at the top and bottom of stairs.

"I saved the special things that my children played with and wore. Then, when my daughters had *their* baby showers, I washed and ironed them and presented each of them with a box of their own baby clothes. Last Christmas, my second granddaughter wore her mom's first Christmas dress. I had made it from red velveteen with a white pique, lace-trimmed collar."

—*Anne Ridgely*

Child gates are great but they don't substitute for good old-fashioned watching (and playing with) your child.

"When Matthew was two, his legs were restless when he was going to bed. I had a habit of holding his foot in my hand and rubbing it gently. It always helped. He is seven now, and occasionally 'hands out' his foot from underneath his blanket if he needs extra comfort or extra attention."

—*Paivi Spoon*

Never try to start potty training until the child can walk.

"My mother always would put Cheerios in the 'big potty.' Then the little boys would aim for the ring."

—*Shirley Posten*

You don't see many kindergarteners wearing diapers. They will get it, just when they want to!

Sleepwalking or talking in their sleep may be a sign that the child needs to go to the bathroom and just isn't awake enough to realize it. Steer them in the right direction and they'll take care of themselves.

"We used the bribery technique to potty train our daughter and it worked very well. She got a star sticker every time she used the potty. Ten stickers and she got a new My Little Pony. Three new My Little Ponies and she was trained."

—*Maxine Como*

The classic potty training book is Once Upon a Potty *by Alana Frankel. Be prepared to read this book almost as many times as you read* Good Night, Moon.

"I was told by a friend that in other countries children were allowed to run around naked while they toilet trained. When it came time to start this process with my first born, we went with this method. I explained to my son that we do not go 'pee-pee' on the floor. As he was not wearing clothes or a diaper, I was hoping he had no choice but to use the potty seats strategically placed throughout the house. As I was cooking dinner one evening, my naked two-and-a-half year old ran into the kitchen and pulled the wet/dry Dust Buster off the wall. I watched as he ran to the living room and proceeded to vacuum up 'pee-pee.' This method of toilet training obviously works better where two-and-a-half year olds don't have access to wet/dry vacs."

—*Susan Cross*

Always buckle up your child and yourself before you start the car. That way they understand from the earliest age that the car won't start until all are safely in their seat belts.

Children should always ride in the back seat. It's the safest place.

"Remember for child care that any amount of money to put your mind at ease is money well spent."

—Kirsten Burton

As They Grow

Though I live in Scotland and my mother is in Texas, the miles that separate us make no difference. I have tried to take her teachings and use them to understand others and myself. I feel these teachings have given me the ability to stand on my own, independent, strong, and with the peace of mind that I shall always do my very best. I am my mother in many ways, and when I look into my daughter's wee eyes I see myself, and my own mother, and know that we are all connected, we are all one."

—*Bobbie Isbell*

Listen to your child. Learn her rhythm and respect it. If your child is quiet, be prepared to slow down your approach. If you have a boisterous child, a little roughhousing is allowed. Don't try and force your wishes on your child.

You don't learn from your successes, you learn from your mistakes.

"My mother said, 'Children come to live with you, not you to live with them. They are really only with you for a little while. Your job, as a parent, is to help them grow into whole, complete adults who can and do become independent from you!' This is a hard lesson to learn, but a necessary one to keep things in perspective."

—*Mary Jane Kolar*

"I can remember when I was little, maybe three or four years old, being held close to my mom. I remember falling asleep, and feeling very safe."
—*Mabel Thompson*

Find the child in yourself and enjoy your young ones.

Looking at the world through a child's eyes is like seeing it all over again.

"Every Mother's Day I write a letter to each of my children telling them how I am feeling. Sometimes I write about the new things they learned that week or how they drove me nuts with their crankiness. I want them to read these letters when they get older and I hope they realize that things weren't always perfect but we managed just fine. I am enjoying every minute with my kids."

—*Jo Anne Sheldrick*

It may seem that your children are always testing you. In reality, they are testing themselves.

"Like many Washingtonians, our families live at a distance. When our children were small, we drove back to St. Louis or down to Tampa at least once a year. To break the monotony I would buy small gifts for each child, which I wrapped and gave out as we crossed into a new state. The gifts were little books, a finger puppet, a small stuffed animal, anything small and entertaining. They looked forward to the surprise and it helped break the tedium. (Ohio was still a pain.) My one real rule : Only one gift per state. My children still talk about how they enjoyed this practice—and they're both in their twenties."

—*Susan Kleimann*

Apologize to your kids when you do something wrong. You'll feel better and it's a great way to show them how they can do it too.

Don't get your kids a dog until they're old enough to take care of it themselves.

"Read to your child from the day she is born until she can read to you. It may be the single greatest gift you can give. My mother and grandmother gave this to me as I have done with my children. And now I'm giving it to my first grandchild."

—*Marita Jane Brown*

Keep track of your child's immunizations with dates, boosters, etc. A child's baby book is a good place for this information. This will come in very handy when they start school. It seems hard to think that far ahead when they're tiny babies, but believe me the day will come when they head out the door with their little backpack and climb on the school bus.

Teach your children the proper way to wash their hands—with plenty of bubbles from the soapy water.

Wash with soap and water four times a day, and keep the pediatrician away.

"Having babies is rough on your hands as you're always washing something. Here's a recipe from my grandmother who was born in 1892. She was famous (at least among family members) for the hand lotion she made. This stuff is great, very moisturizing and soothing. There's no formal name for it—we always called it Grandmother's Hand Lotion."

5 cups water
2 cups bay rum
1 cup witch hazel
1 cup glycerin
½ cup flax seed

Gently boil water and flax seed for five minutes. Strain and add other ingredients, stirring constantly. Add a few drops of red or other food coloring. Add perfume or oil of lavender to the lotion.

—*Ruth E. Pope*

You and your husband will ask each other what you used to do with all the free time you used to have before you had a baby.

Never say you'll never let your kids watch TV. Never say you'll never use the TV as a babysitter. You will, at least a little, and you'll be glad it's there to give you a break. The secret, and it's not much of a secret, is to watch it together, or at least comment on what's going on as you pass through the room.

"My daughter watched *Sesame Street* almost every day and I was right there beside her. Sometimes I would catch myself discussing the characters with her as if they were real. It drove me crazy when it was pledge week and the station would preempt the show to dun the audience for money. My daughter would look at the bank of phone operators and cry inconsolably."

—*Sherry Conway Appel*

Disney videos are great when you need to write out the bills or make a few phone calls. They keep even babies entertained when you need a few minutes of adult life.

"For the toddler who doesn't like to take medicine, here's a trick from my mom. After checking with the doctor/pharmacist, mix the medicine into something your child loves to eat, like ice cream or pudding. Or cut a straw to about two inches long and let them slurp it out of a medicine cup. My mom always has everyone in the house cheer the child on, too, which makes them feel very proud once the medicine is gone."

—*Shirley Posten*

For children with particularly dry or rough skin due to eczema or allergies, put lotion or creams on when their skin is still wet from the bath.

A good way to entice sick children to eat is to serve them pieces of buttered toast cut with cookie cutters.

"When I was young, I always managed to cause trouble when Mom was nursing my baby brother. No matter how many locks or obstacles, I always managed to work my way outside and down the street. So when my second child was born, my mom presented my daughter with a special toy with lots of beads on it. We kept it in the nursery so Kathryn could be occupied while I nursed Tyler, my son. Mom's special toy really works to keep us *all* happy, and really helped me out."

—Julie Gerig

"My sisters and I followed our mother's advice to have two children a year apart. She always said you were going to lose the first couple of years anyway, you might as well double up and save yourself some time in the long run."

—*Eileen Toumanoff*

During your pregnancy with your second child, make an event out of preparing a "new" room for your firstborn (or create a new space in the room if they are to share). Let her pick out the bed or a new bedcover, or make a special lampshade together that's just for her. It will ease the transition when the new baby comes on the scene and grabs most of the attention.

Despite your desire to spend time with them in the evenings, babies and toddlers need sleep. Have them in bed by eight P.M. Keep the regular bedtime, and you won't have getting-to-bed problems later on.

Bedtime rituals are important. Read a book, sing them a song, kiss baby and bear, and then it's lights out.

Don't start the habit of letting your child sleep with you. And no matter how many times your son gets into your bed at night, take him back to his own bed, tuck him in, and kiss him good night. Even though you will be exhausted, after a week he should be broken of his habit and you will be able to sleep through the night again.

"When I was pregnant with my second child, I went in for a standard sonogram. I was hoping it would show I was having a girl because I already had a boy.

"I went to look at the pictures, and it was obvious my baby was a boy. So I asked, 'Is there any way that thing I'm seeing could be anything other than what it appears to be?' The technician laughed and said, 'No way.'

"So I called my mother to seek some sympathy. She thought for a moment, knowing she had to say something comforting and uplifting, and replied, 'You know what, Robin? This is actually a blessing in disguise. Now you can get bunk beds.'"

—*Robin Latham*

Don't buy really good furniture until the kids are old enough to keep from ruining it. Or if you do, keep the good stuff in a room that isn't used very much.

"One of the best things my mother did for my brother, sister, and me was to write down the stories of her childhood and our own that we traditionally told again and again. I remember her stories about Millie, the pony who would hide in the pasture when it was time to come in, or Bud, the sheepdog who wouldn't go outside in snow and ice unless he had his little boots on. From my childhood, I remember the squirrel that ran up our Christmas tree and the chaos of trying to get him out of the house. But my mother wrote these down and saved them for her children and grandchildren. It is such a gift."

—*Susan Kleimann*

Just remember to have patience, especially during
those moments when you need ten hands.

"Lower your standards. The need for a clean and safe house remains; the need for a showcase beautiful house is too much. A simple house is easy to clean. I stuck with bare floors and a dust mop, plus that old hotel maid standby for the bathrooms—a towel to dry everything off right away and lots of bluing in the toilet tank. Leave rolls of paper towels all over to wipe spills down right away.

"Keep in mind the old WWI adage—don't worry about the war, just make it to the next trench. The good news is that whatever is driving you nuts will quickly pass as the kids go on to new and more complicated things.

"Always remember, it is a wonderful, awesome, scary responsibility that will have you worrying about your children from age zero till your last day, but it is part of the greatest gift that one can have, and binds you forever in the great chain of life and humanity."

—*Teresa Chin Jones*

You'll always feel guilty about something.

You'll always worry about them.

You'll never have enough energy.

You'll never have enough time.

You'll always love them.

"Spoil your children, rock them, tell them bedtime stories, tell them over and over how beautiful and great they are. I have done this with my daughter and we are very close. She is bright, beautiful, and strong."

—*Mimi Baudoin*

Acknowledgments

$\mathcal{I}$ would like to thank the following women for contributing their stories, ideas, and wisdom to this book. Motherhood can be the most joyous time in a woman's life. I am fortunate that these women could share their insights, wonder, and experience for all new mothers in need of a helping hand.

Irene Appel; Catherine Babb, Deborah Hand; Mimi Baudoin, Zola Baudoin, Michelle Pries; Beth Bester; Donna Greenfield Belser, Mikell Belser,

Lauren Belser, Pearl Teich Greenfield; Sally Brickman; Leah Marie Brown, Faith Brown; Marita Jane Brown, Marita Curtin Bisceglia, Peter Neily Brown; Kirsten Burton, Lila Wengler; Maxine Como; Susan Cross, Mary Catherine Walker, Sydney Cross, Shelby Cross; Louisa Davis, Renee Davis, Tonya Davis; Susan De Wit; Sandy Appel Fisher, Amanda Fisher, Emma Fisher; Alison Frank; Sally Games; Julie Himes Gerig, Kathryn Conway Gerig; Rasheeda Gilmore, Stephanie Gilmore; Lynne Glassman, Muriel Woronov, Samantha Lynne Glassman; Joy Goins, Monica Chaney, Blake Peterman; Victoria Harper, Shelly Heller, Deborah Herr, Tracey Herr, Heather Herr; Susan Conway Himes, Helen Leona Conway; Bobbie Isbell; Edmina Janus; Teresa Chin Jones; Stacy Jordan, Almeda Jordan, Kiara Jordan; Lorrie Kahaner; Susan Kleimann, Dorothy Trybula, Kristin Kleimann; Mary Jane Kolar, Mary S. Burnett;

Robin Latham, Sarah Levey; Jean Kelly McCall; Ann Maristows; Christine Middleton, Lillian Bass, McKinsey Lyn Middleton; Suzanne Nowell, Riley Nowell, Reagan Nowell; Juanita Patterson; Ann Wagner Pellerin, Marion L. Wagner; Ruth E. Pope; Shirley Posten, Paula Hanson, Abigail Posten, Miranda Posten; Lavonne Proctor, Shavonne Proctor; Linda Ours Rago, Bessie Lee Hartman Ours, Lulu Catherine Davy Hartman; Cina Radler, Brody Letson; Anne Ridgely, Dorothy Fleming, Jennifer DuLaney, Katherine Thomas; Marilyn Rybak, Marilene Hardisty, Gertrude Elizabeth Moler; Jo Anne Sheldrick, Arlene Korteweg; Beverly Silverberg, Nina Silverberg; Paivi Spoon, Irja Verho; Regina Fraind Smith, Stefany Novak Fraind; Tonya Stewart, Bernadette Shaw; Dina Tabbah, Carina Tabbah; April Thomas, Katherine Lewis, Rachel Thomas; Mabel Thompson, Bessie Thompson, Jackie Thompson;

Eileen Toumanoff, Louise MacVeagh, Nina Toumanoff; Mary Catherine Walker, Mary Lou Park Nemir; Beverly Warfield, Jessica Warfield, Christine Warfield; Tracy Wilgus Weins, Sadie Jane Weins, Mattie Kay Weins, Judy Conway Wilgus; Leanne Whiteman, Roberta Whiteman; Linda Wilson; Sunday Wynkoop, Susan Hammett, Carrie Wynkoop Neuman.